Little Skill Seekers

NUMBERS & COUNTING

SCHOLASTIC

New York • Toronto • London • Auckland • Sydney • New Delhi
Mexico City • Hong Kong • Buenos Aires

Cover Design: Tannaz Fassihi
Cover Illustration: Michael Robertson
Interior Design: Mina Chen
Interior Illustration: Doug Jones

ISBN: 978-1-338-25554-6
Copyright © Scholastic Inc. All rights reserved. Printed in the U.S.A.
First printing, June 2018.

2 3 4 5 6 7 8 9 10   40   24 23 22 21 20

Dear Parent,

Welcome to *Little Skill Seekers: Numbers & Counting*! Numeral identification and number sense are the basis for more advanced math concepts—this workbook will help your child develop these skills.

Help your little skill seeker build a strong foundation for learning by choosing more books in the Little Skill Seekers series. The exciting and colorful workbooks in the series are designed to set your child on the path to success. Each book targets essential skills important to your child's development.

Here are some key features of *Little Skill Seekers: Numbers & Counting* and the other workbooks in this series:

- Filled with colorful illustrations that make learning fun and playful

- Provides plenty of opportunity to practice essential skills

- Builds independence as children work through the pages on their own, at their own pace

- Comes in a perfect size that fits easily in a backpack for practice on the go

Now let's get started on this journey to help your child become a successful, lifelong learner!

—The Editors

Color the number.

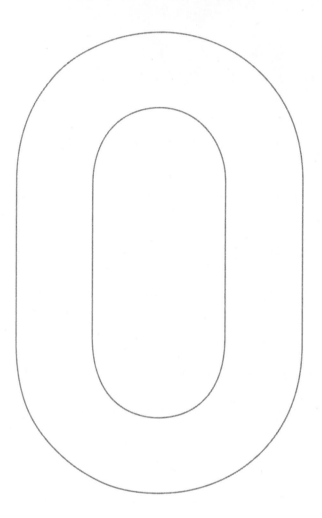

Trace and write 0.

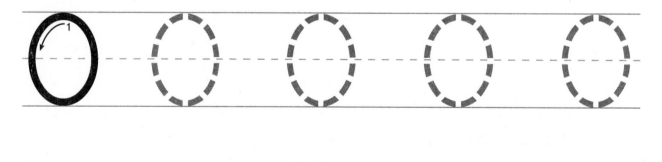

How many penguins do you see in the picture?

Color one square for each penguin you see.

☐ ☐ ☐ ☐ ☐ ☐ ☐ ☐ ☐ ☐

Trace and write zero.

Color the number.

Trace and write .

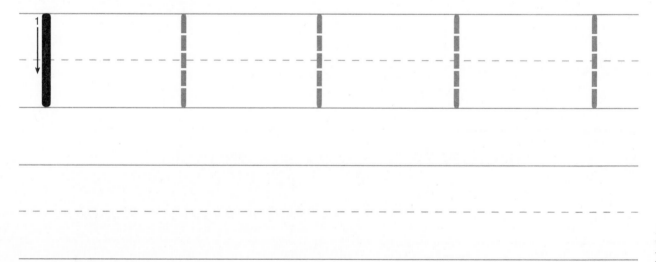

How many bees do you see in the picture?

Color one square for each bee you see.

Trace and write one.

one

Write the number that comes before 1.

| | 1 |

Color the number.

Trace and write 2.

2 2 2 2 2

How many birds do you see in the picture?

Color one square for each bird you see.

Trace and write two.

two

Write the numbers that come before 2.

Circle each group of 1.

Circle each group of 2.

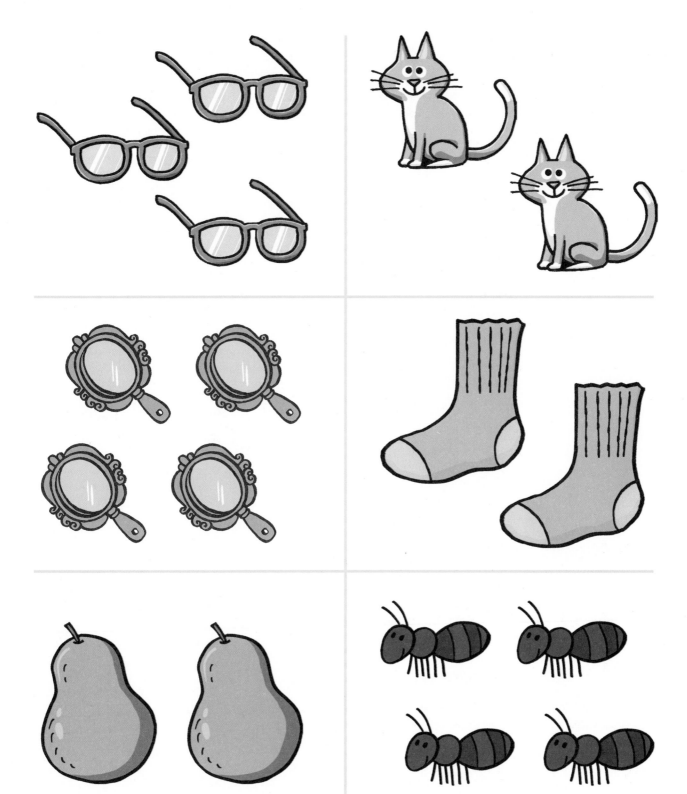

Color the number.

Trace and write 3.

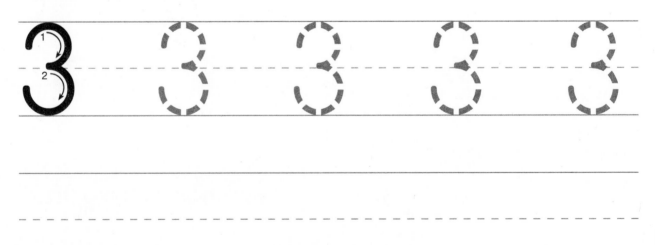

How many mice do you see in the picture?

Color one square for each mouse you see.

Trace and write three.

three

Write the numbers that come before 3.

Color the number.

Trace and write 4.

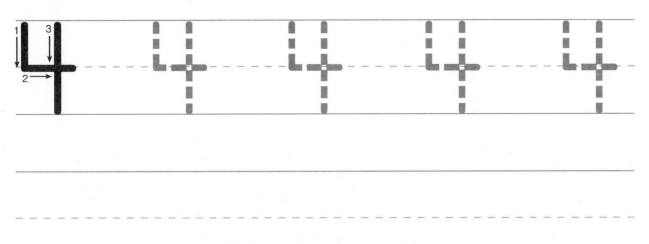

How many fish do you see in the picture?

Color one square for each fish you see.

Trace and write four.

Write the numbers that come before 4.

				4

Circle each group of 3.

Circle each group of 4.

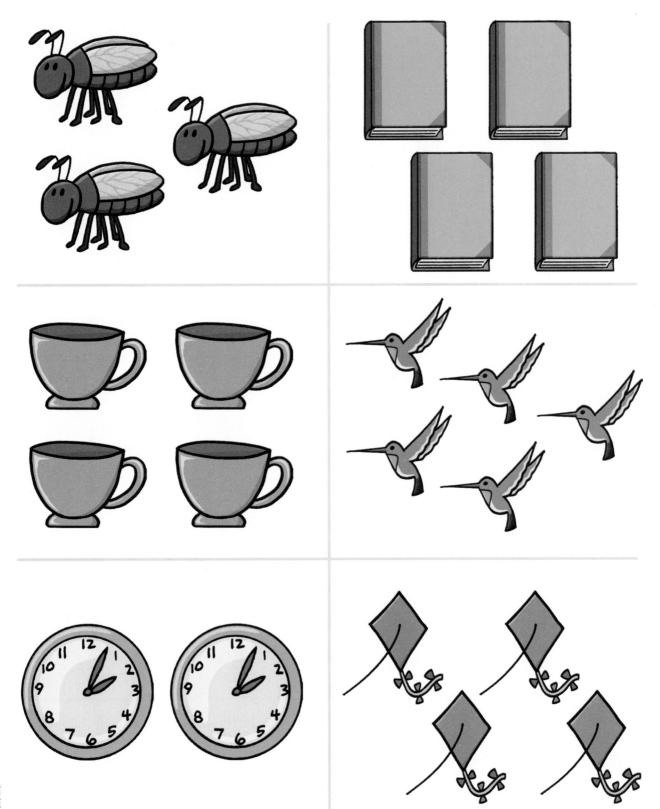

Color the number.

Trace and write 5.

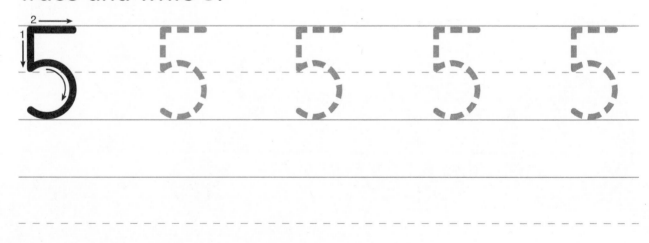

How many stars do you see in the picture?

Color one square for each star you see.

Trace and write five.

Write the numbers that come before 5.

					5

Color the number.

Trace and write 6.

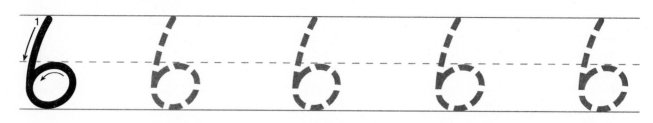

How many ducks do you see in the picture?

Color one square for each duck you see.

Trace and write six.

Write the numbers that come before 6.

Circle each group of 5.

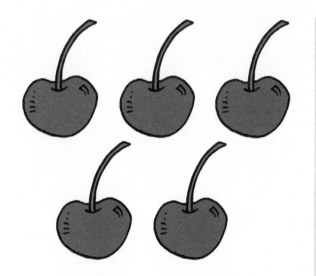

Circle each group of 6.

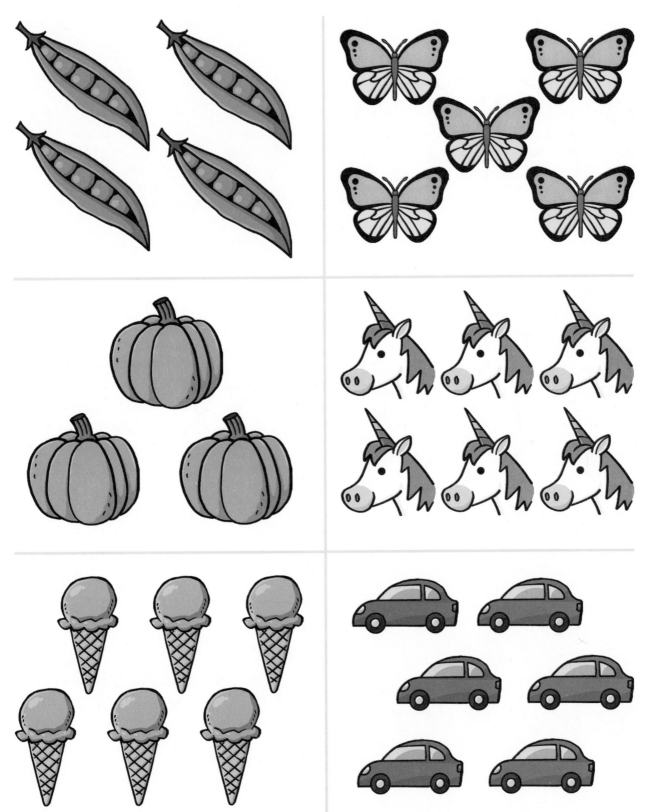

Write the missing numbers.

Match each group with the same number of items.

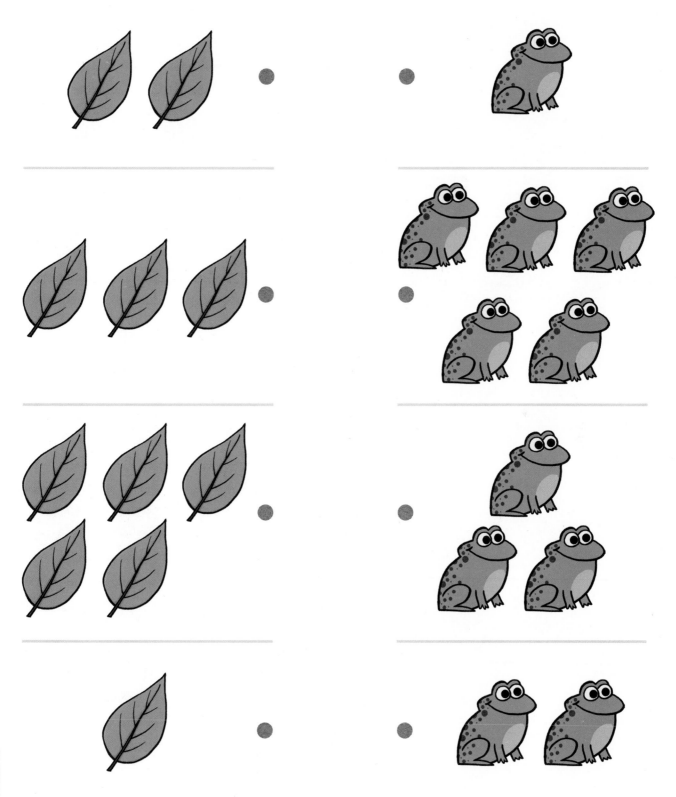

Count the items in each set.
Circle the number.

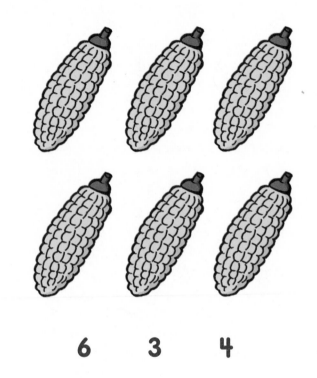

3   1   2   6   3   4

5   1   2   4   3   5

Help the girl get to the house.
Follow the numbers. Draw a line from 0 to 6.

Count the items in each set.
Match each set with the correct number.

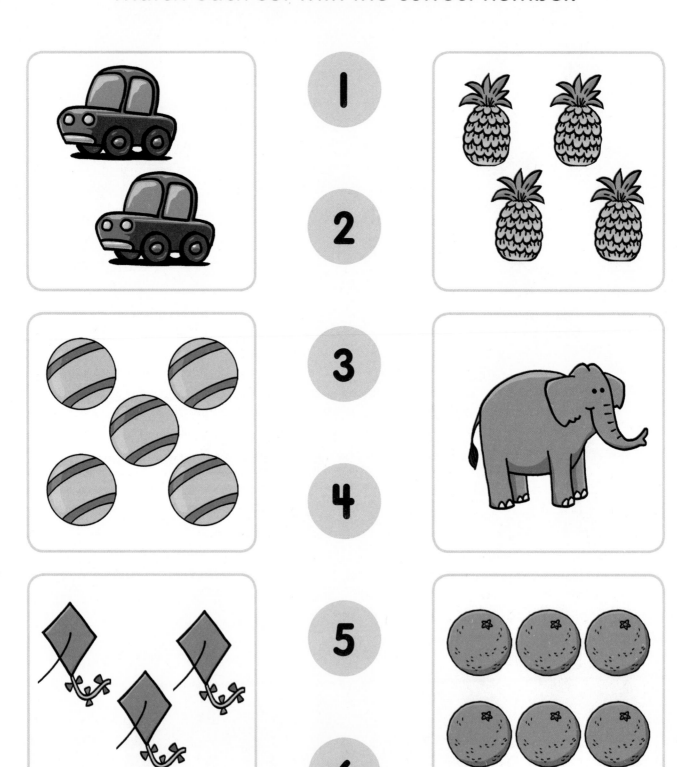

Count the items in each set.
Write the number in the box.

Color the number.

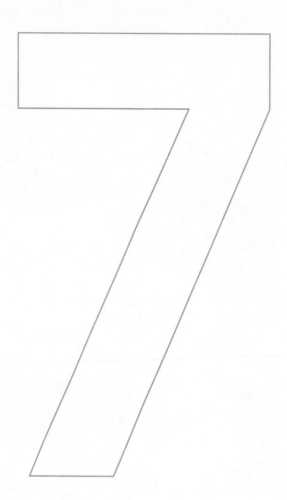

Trace and write 7.

How many buildings do you see in the picture?

Color one square for each building you see.

Trace and write seven.

seven

Write the numbers that come before 7.

7

Color the number.

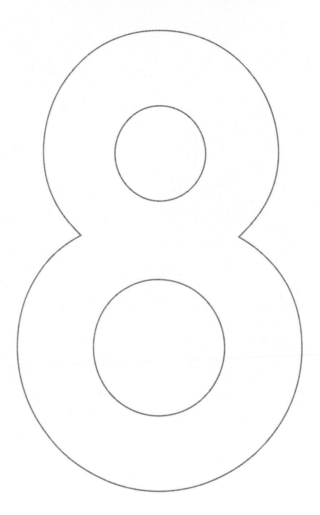

Trace and write 8.

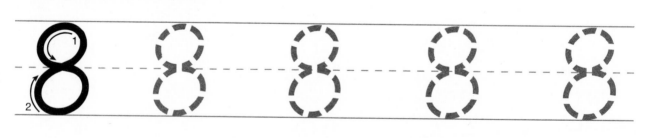

How many seahorses do you see in the picture?

Color one square for each seahorse you see.

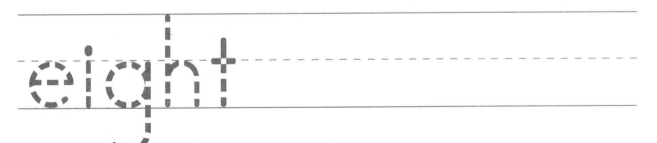

Trace and write eight.

eight

Write the numbers that come before 8.

 8

Circle each group of 7.

Circle each group of 8.

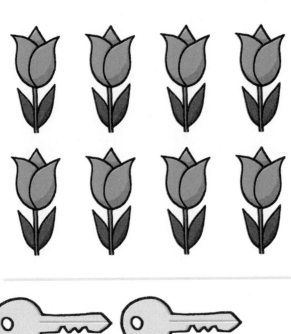 

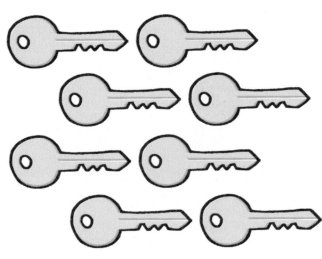 

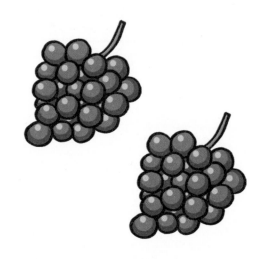 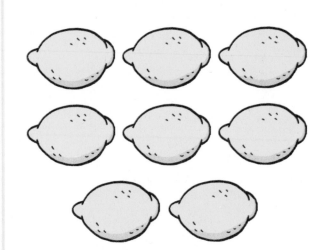

Color the number.

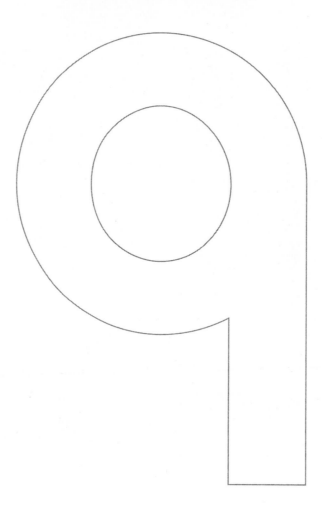

Trace and write 9.

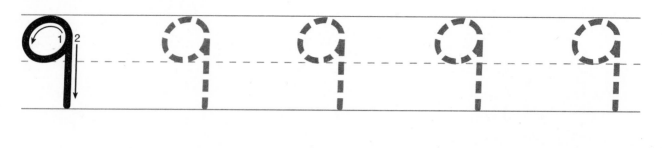

How many shells do you see in the picture?

Color one square for each shell you see.

☐ ☐ ☐ ☐ ☐ ☐ ☐ ☐ ☐ ☐

Trace and write nine.

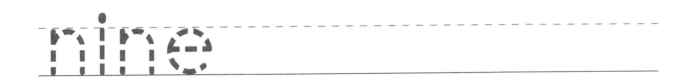

Write the numbers that come before 9.

Color the number.

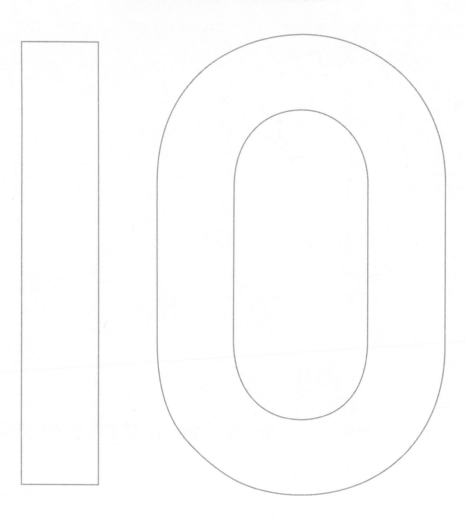

Trace and write 10.

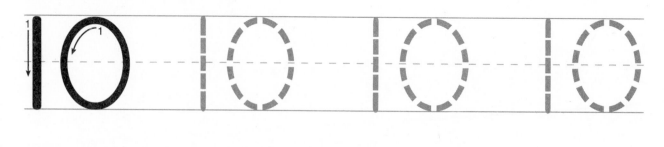

How many balloons do you see in the picture?

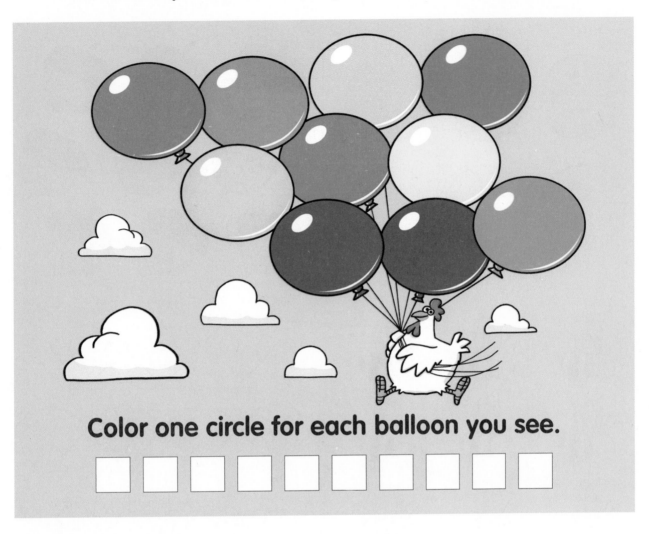

Color one circle for each balloon you see.

Trace and write ten.

t̶e̶n̶

Write the numbers that come before 10.

 10

Circle each group of 9.

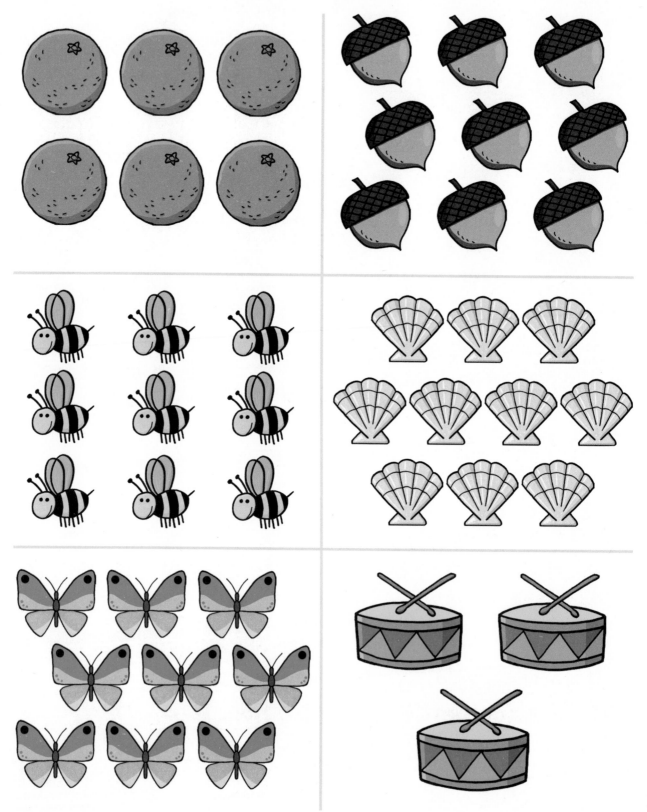

Circle each group of 10.

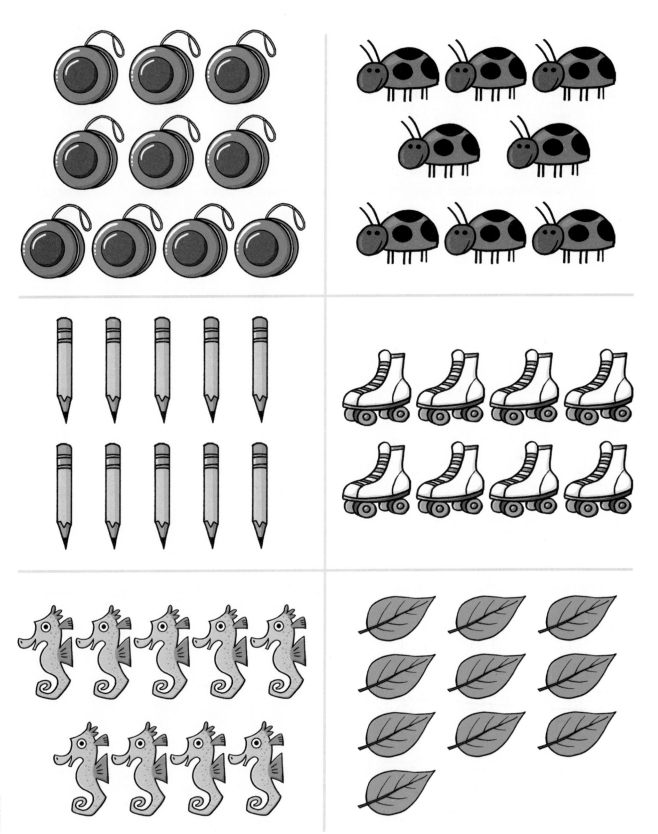

Write the missing numbers.

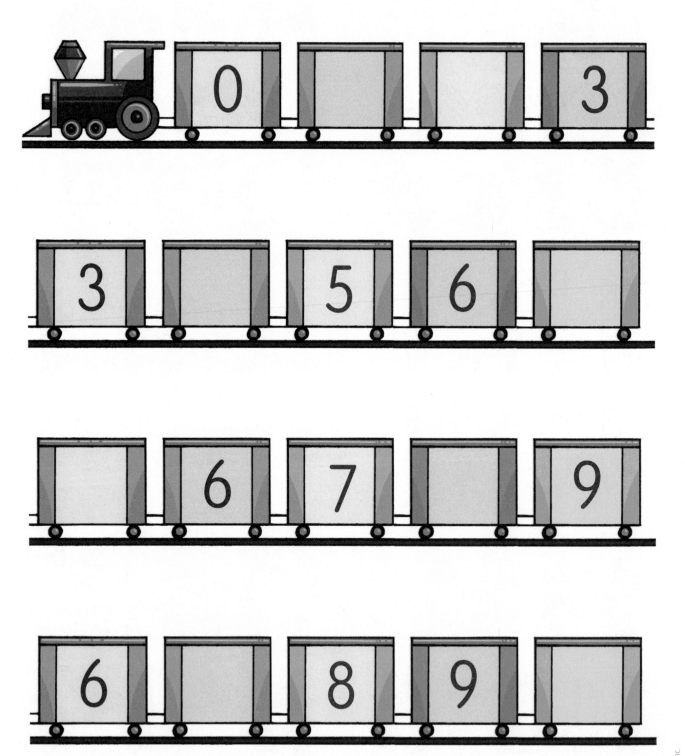

Match each group with the same number of items.

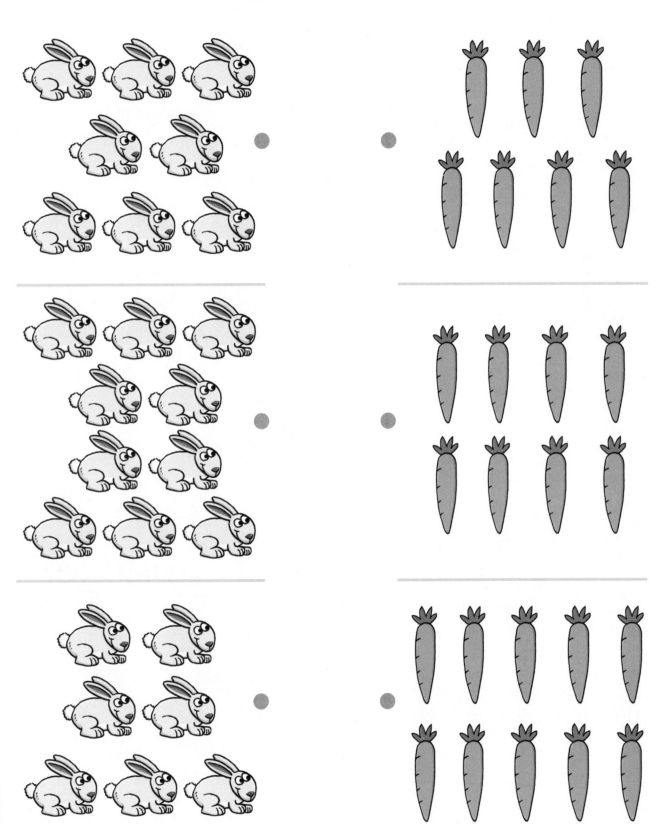

Count the items in each set.
Circle the number.

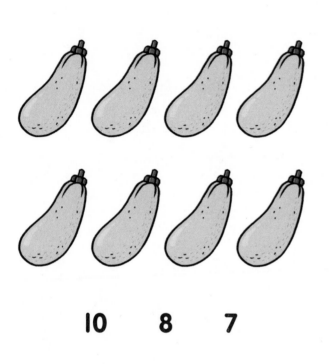

10   8   7

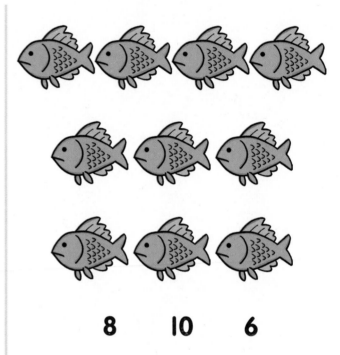

8   10   6

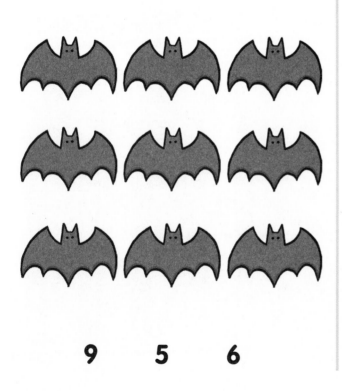

9   5   6

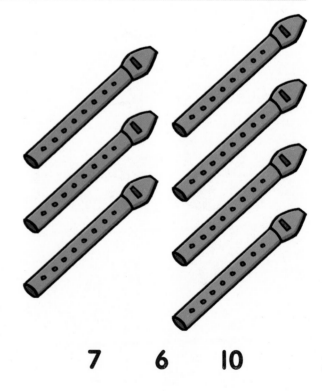

7   6   10

Help the boy find his skateboard.
Follow the numbers. Draw a line from 0 to 8.

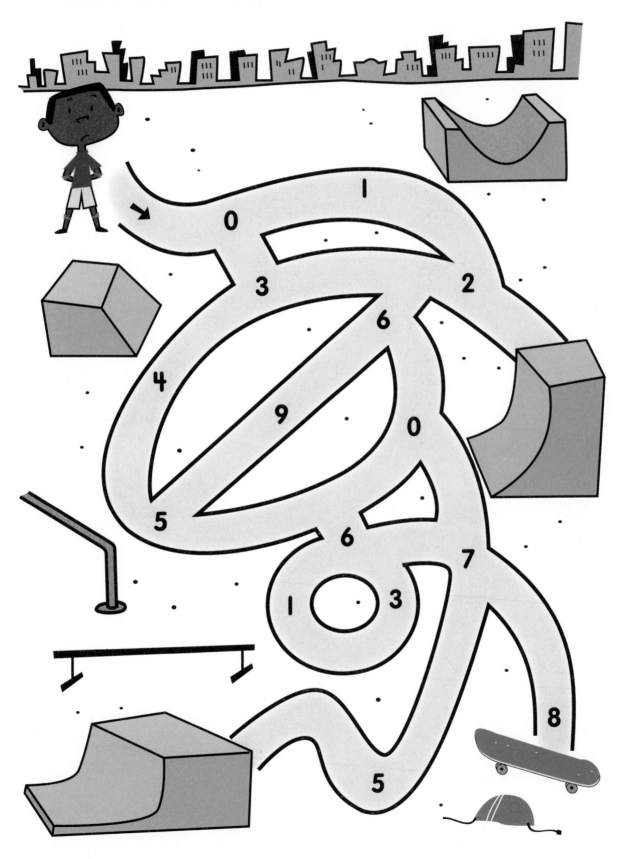

Count the items in each set.
Match each set with the correct number.

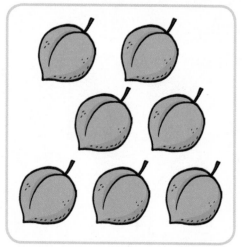

1

2

3

4

5

6

7

8

9

10

Count the items in each set.
Write the number in the box.

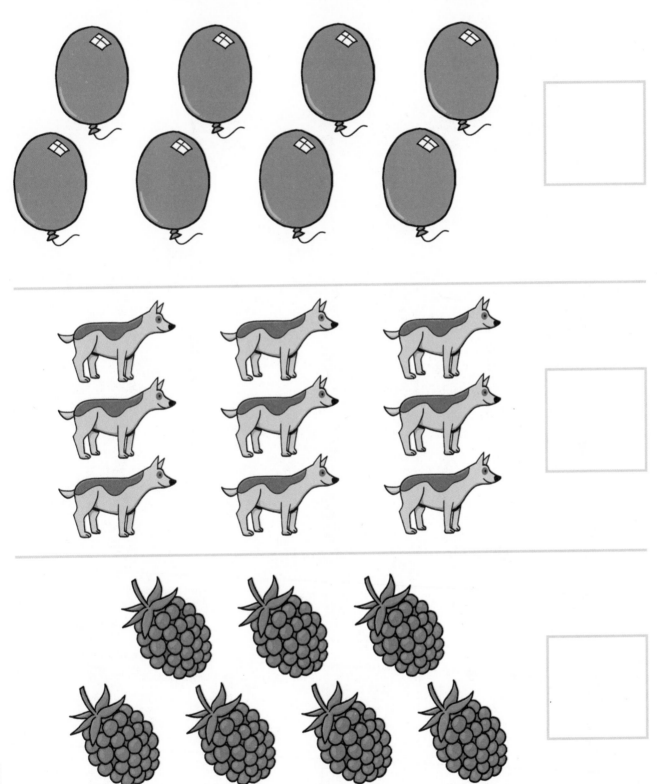

Help the boy find his pail and shovel.
Follow the numbers. Draw a line from 0 to 10.